MACHINES RULE!

ON THE
BUILDING SITE

Steve Parker

A⁺

Smart Apple Media

Smart Apple Media
P.O. Box 3263
Mankato, Minnesota 56002

Printed in the United States.

Published by arrangement with the Watts Publishing
Group Ltd, London.

Library of Congress Cataloging-in-Publication Data

Parker, Steve, 1976-
  On the building site / Steve Parker.
      p. cm.—(Machines rule!)
  Includes bibliographical references and index.
  Summary: "Covers a wide selection of construction machines,
  outlining how they work and what they are used for"
  —Provided by publisher.
  ISBN 978-1-59920-288-4 (hardcover)
  1. Building sites—Juvenile literature. 2. Landscape
construction—Juvenile literature. 3. Earthwork—Juvenile literature.
  4. Earthmoving machinery—Juvenile literature. I. Title.
  TH380.P37 2010
  690.028'4–dc22
                                                    2008044499

Editor: Jeremy Smith
Design: Billin Design Solutions
Art director: Jonathan Hair
Picture credits: Alamy: 11all. Shutterstock: OFC all, 2, 3,
6-7 all,8-9 all, 11c, 12-13 all, 14-15 all,16-17 all, 18-19 all,
20-21 all,22-23 all, 24-25 all, 26-27 all.

Words in **bold** or ***bold italics*** can be found in the glossary
on page 28.

9 8 7 6 5 4 3 2 1

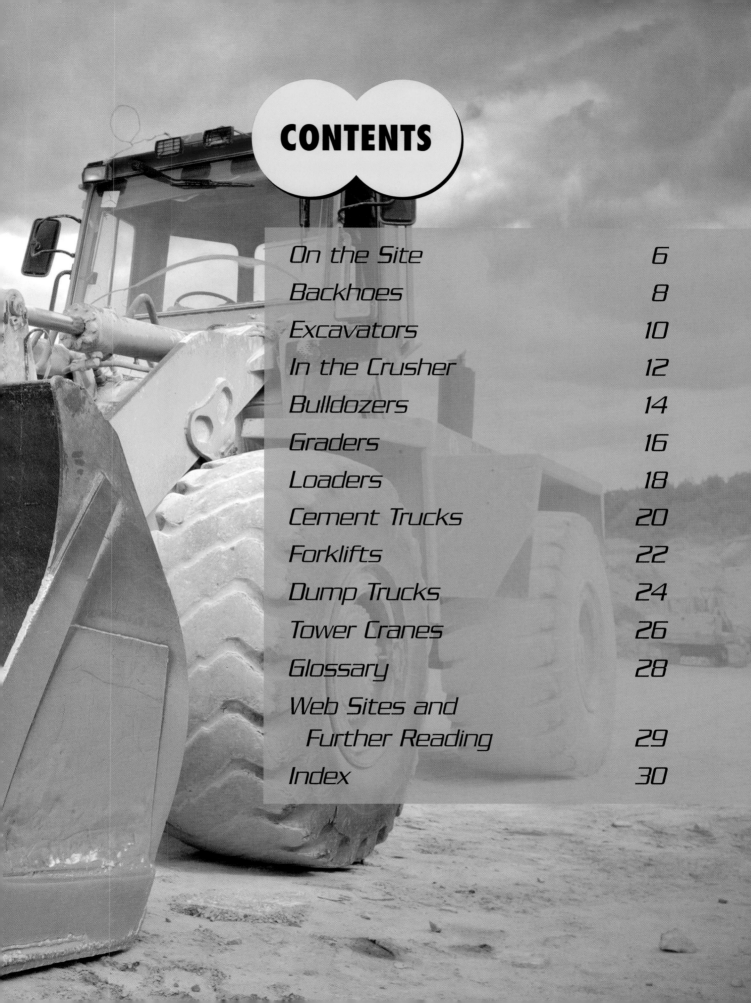

CONTENTS

On the Site

The building site is never dull. Engines roar as backhoes, bulldozers, and other massive machines use their strength. Trucks come and go nonstop, bringing supplies and materials. Time is money, so rain hardly slows the pace—it just creates more mud!

Do-It-All Diggers
Backhoes don't just scoop earth. They lift and move loose materials such as sand, gravel, rocks, and rubble, as well as packs of bricks and blocks. Like all construction machines, they are strong, tough, and reliable.

Driving Dozers

When push comes to shove, bulldozers can't be beaten. Their shiny **blades** and crawler tracks flatten rough ground, shift piles of materials, and can even level out a hill.

What a Dump!

Dump trucks are the workhorses of the building trade. They carry anything from muddy dirt to new doors and window frames. Loaders fill them up, and off they go again.

Bird's Eye View

High in the sky, the crane operator has the best view as the building takes shape. The driver's phone is always busy with requests to move things. But it's a long way up to the **cab**—and a long way down to the bathroom!

Backhoes

Before you start to build up, you need to dig down! Backhoes are among the first machines at a building site. They scoop out holes for a building's base and make space for the foundations or footings.

Backhoes have crawlers, or **caterpillar tracks**. These help to spread the huge weight and grip well in mud. You could fit six people in the backhoe's bucket!

THAT'S INCREDIBLE

Teams of "dancing diggers" (backhoes) from the United Kingdom give shows and displays, moving to music like massive mechanical dancers.

JS 130L Tracked Excavator (backhoe)

Maker: JCB (USA)

Length: 25 ft (7.6 m), arm folded

Width: 8.9 ft (2.7 m) across tracks

Height: 8.9 ft (2.7 m) to top of cab

Weight: 15 tons (14 t)

Digging Height: Up to 29 ft (8.8 m)

Digging Forward Reach: 26 ft (7.9 m)

Digging Depth: Down to 16.7 ft (5.1 m)

Engine: Isuzu A4BGIT (4.3 L) turbo diesel

Speed: 3.4 mph (5.5 km/h)

Some backhoes have tires with extra deep ridges, or **tread**, so they don't get stuck in the ground.

Smaller backhoes can fit into some gardens. They can churn soil 100 times faster than a person with a spade.

Excavators

Excavators do really big digging jobs. Dragline excavators are some of the biggest. Some can have buckets as big as buses! They are used in quarries and mines, as well as for building roads and railroads.

THAT'S INCREDIBLE

The world's biggest land vehicle is the Krupp Bagger 288 Bucket-Wheel Mining Excavator. It weighs 50,155 tons (45,500 t)—more than many ocean liners.

The dragline excavator swings its bucket out and down on one steel cable. It then drags the bucket back using another cable, or line, to scrape up earth.

Huge excavators are used to hollow out hills filled with valuable things such as coal, minerals, and gemstones.

Bucyrus 8200 Walking Dragline Excavator

Maker: Bucyrus (USA)

Weight: More than 4,409 tons (4,000 tonnes)

Boom Length: Up to 400 ft (122 m)

Bucket Size: Up to 3,108 ft^3 (88 m^3)

Power: Electric motors

Load Weight: Up to 187 tons (170 t)

Dig Depth: 144 ft (44 m)

Dig to Dump Distance: 656 ft (200 m)

Dump Height: 148 ft (45 m)

There are different buckets for various jobs. A narrow bucket digs, or hoes, a thin trench.

The wheels and **gears** of giant dragline excavators must be constantly oiled to make sure they keep working properly.

In the Crusher

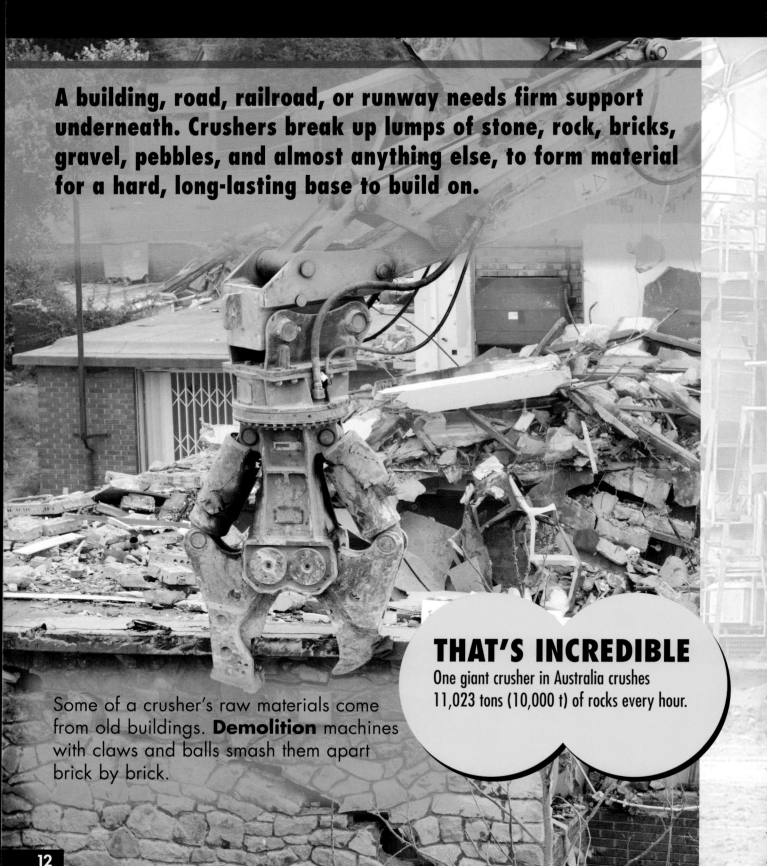

A building, road, railroad, or runway needs firm support underneath. Crushers break up lumps of stone, rock, bricks, gravel, pebbles, and almost anything else, to form material for a hard, long-lasting base to build on.

Some of a crusher's raw materials come from old buildings. **Demolition** machines with claws and balls smash them apart brick by brick.

THAT'S INCREDIBLE
One giant crusher in Australia crushes 11,023 tons (10,000 t) of rocks every hour.

Crushers take in all kinds of rock-hard items at one end and pour out smaller pieces at the other end. This rubble is great for making building materials.

Broken pieces of rock and rubble pour off the end of the crusher's **conveyor belt**.

Nordberg/Lokotrack LT1213S Mobile Crusher

Maker: Metso Nordberg (Finland)

Crusher unit: Nordberg NP1213

Feeder unit: TK11-42-2V vibrating feeder

Length for Transport: 56.4 ft (17.2 m)

Width for Transport: 9.8 ft (3 m)

Height for Transport: 11.2 ft (3.4 m)

Weight: 52.4 tons (47.5 t)

Feed Hopper Volume: 318 ft^3 (9 m^3)

Feed Hopper Size: 13.5 ft by 3.6 ft (4.1 m by 1.1 m)

Size of Crushed Pieces: .79 in–2.75 in (20 mm–70 mm)

Bulldozers

The bulldozer's steel blade is raised and lowered by hydraulic pistons.

If it's pushing or pulling power you need, use a bulldozer! This is the heaviest and slowest machine on many building sites. Its main job is to scrape and push surfaces flat and level.

The driver turns the bulldozer by making the caterpillar track on one side move faster than the track on the other side.

Caterpillar D9

Maker: Caterpillar (USA)

Length: 26.6 ft (8.1 m)

Blade Width: 14.8 ft (4.5 m)

Height: 13.1 ft (4 m)

Weight: 54 tons (49 t)

Engine: CAT C18 (18 L) ACERT turbocharged diesel

Power: More than 500 horsepower

Forward Speed: 7.5 mph (12 km/h)

Reverse Speed: 8.7 mph (14 km/h)

The metal ridges on the caterpillar tracks grip very well. They are moved by big gears that have teeth around their edges.

THAT'S INCREDIBLE

The Komatsu D155W bulldozer works underwater, to move and flatten the sea bed around harbors and ports. It is remote-controlled.

Some bulldozers have a claw or **ripper** at the back. As they move along, the ripper tears up and loosens hard ground, even tar and **concrete**.

ripper

Graders

Sometimes people need a smooth area like a lawn, sports field, park, or leveled-off building site. Machines like graders and steamrollers make the ground as flat as a pancake.

blade

Graders can't push massive piles like bulldozers can. But they can make a really flat, even surface by using their wide blades with adjustable height and tilt.

THAT'S INCREDIBLE

When building a new freeway, a team of graders can level the area of a football field in less than two minutes.

Stats and Facts

Model 1450 Grader

Maker: Leon (Canada)

Type: Towed

Length: 27.6 ft (8.4 m)

Width: 9.5 ft (2.9 m)

Width of Cut: 8.5 ft (2.6 m)

Weight: 6 tons (5.5 t)

Power: 425 horsepower

Clearance Above Ground Level: 10.2 inches (26 cm)

Depth of Cut: 11 inches (28 cm)

Rollers are used to make the ground level.

Different blades can be attached to most types of tractors, and are used on everything from open fields to busy roads.

Loaders

There are endless heavy loads to lift around a building site, from earth and rocks to bricks, blocks, and pipes. The loader picks them up and moves them.

A massive bucket scoops up loose soil, sand, gravel, and rubble a few tons at a time. This load is heading for the dump truck.

This claw-like clamp picks up logs and lengths of wood.

THAT'S INCREDIBLE

The Le Tourneau L-2350 is a giant loader weighing 284 tons (258 t) that can lift more than 80 tons (72 t).

Stats and Facts

Volvo L120E Front loader

Maker: Volvo (Sweden)

Length: 26.2 ft (8 m)

Width: 8.9 ft (2.7 m)

Height: 10.8 ft (3.3 m) to cab roof

Weight: Up to 22 tons (20 t)

Engine: D7D LA E2 (7 L) 6 cylinder turbo diesel

Power: 224 horsepower

Bucket Height: 13 ft (4 m)

Top Speed: 22 mph (35 km/h)

Teeth slice in easily to pick up the load.

engine

lights for night work

steps up to the cab

The heavy diesel engine at the back balances the load at the front, so the vehicle doesn't tip forward.

Cement Trucks

"The cement truck is here, everyone grab a shovel!"
When already-mixed concrete arrives, there's
not a moment to lose. As soon as it's poured, it
starts to harden and set.
Every minute counts!

The cement truck contains a load of concrete. As long
as the drum keeps churning around, the load will not
start to harden.

Before starting work, the cement
truck goes to a factory where
massive containers of sand, cement,
and gravel are kept, ready to mix
the next load.

Big loads of concrete pour into trenches to make firm foundations, or footings, for the main walls and girders.

A crane lifts a bulk-load bucket to the upper floors of a tall building. The concrete will flow out of the bottom.

O'Long Concrete Cement Truck

Maker: Steyr/O'Long/Zhongtong (China)

Length: 29.8 ft (9.1 m)

Width: 7.9 ft (2.4 m)

Height: 12.1 ft (3.7 m)

Weight Empty: 14.1 tons (12.8 t)

Engine: Weichai ED615 9.7 L, 6 cylinder gasoline

Power: 360 horsepower

Drum Volume: 318 ft^3 (9 m^3)

Load Weight: Up to 11.8 tons (10.7 t)

Speed: 48 mph (77 km/h)

THAT'S INCREDIBLE

Truck-mounted concrete pumps can push the concrete up through the tube-shaped **boom** to a height of more than 65 yards (60 m).

Forklifts

Building sites, factories, warehouses, and ports all use forklifts to lift and move large goods around.

THAT'S INCREDIBLE
Many countries have forklift competitions that include unloading a truck in the fastest, neatest way and driving through an obstacle course.

Big diesel-engined forklifts work at ports and distribution centers. They raise standard-sized steel cargo **containers** up onto trucks, ships, and railroad cars.

This forklift has a long **boom** at the front that can extend up and out to reach and move loads around.

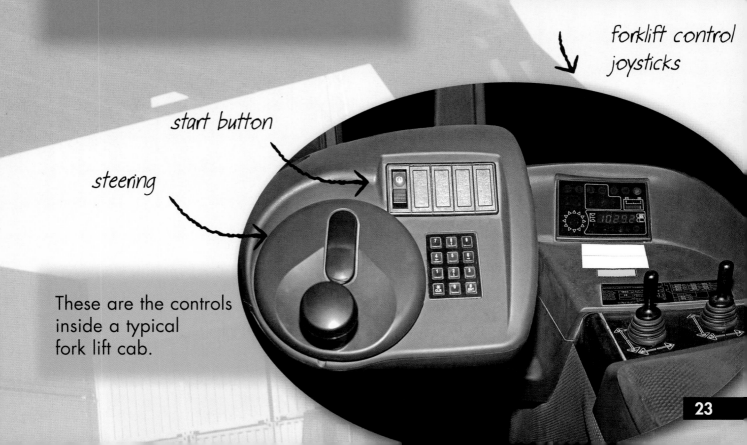

forklift control joysticks

start button

steering

These are the controls inside a typical fork lift cab.

Dump Trucks

Dump trucks come in all shapes and sizes. Some are so massive they could hold a whole house! They carry all kinds of loose materials, from clean sand to demolition debris.

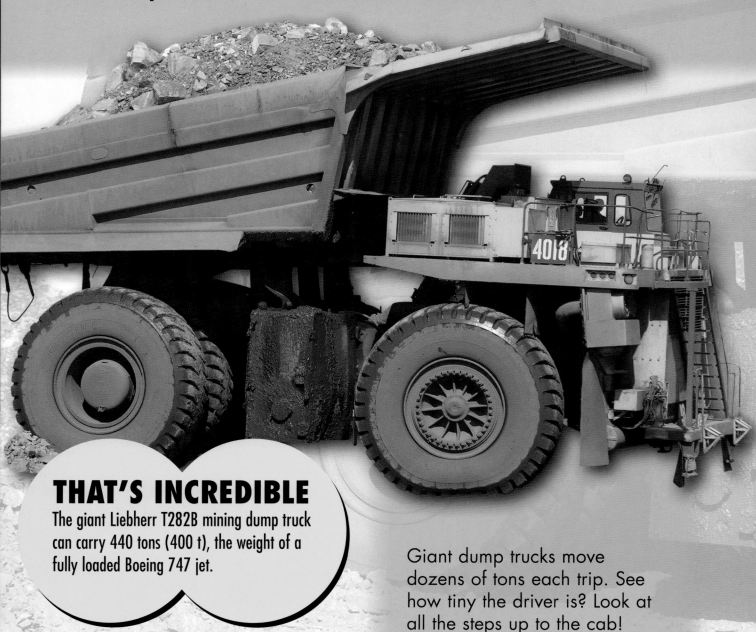

THAT'S INCREDIBLE
The giant Liebherr T282B mining dump truck can carry 440 tons (400 t), the weight of a fully loaded Boeing 747 jet.

Giant dump trucks move dozens of tons each trip. See how tiny the driver is? Look at all the steps up to the cab!

Some trucks can tip their loads backward and to one side. There's also a crane grab to scoop out loose loads or lift heavy items.

The power to tilt comes from hydraulic pistons, which raise the front of the body so it hinges or pivots near the back.

piston

730

Actros Bluetec 4 8x4 Dump Truck

Maker: Mercedes-Benz (Germany)

Length: 28.5 ft (8.7 m)

Width: 7.9 ft (2.4 m)

Height: 10.5 ft (3.2 m) to cab roof

Empty Weight: 10.8 tons (9.8 t)

Load: 35 tons (32 t)

Engine: Mercedes-Benz OM501LA 12 L, V6 turbo diesel

Power: 435 Horsepower

Gearbox: 16-speed (8 high, 8 low)

Top Speed: 63 mph (102 km/h)

Tower Cranes

For tall buildings, you need tall cranes. The tower crane is always busy on site. It lifts, swings, and lowers all kinds of loads.

THAT'S INCREDIBLE

The biggest tower cranes can lift and lower loads of 110 tons (100 t) anywhere over an area of six football fields.

The crane operator has a long climb to work each day! Inside there's a radio link for talking to people on the ground about what needs moving next.

Workers bolt extra sections of the tower in place to make it taller. The crane lifts up its own sections, which fit one inside the other.

counterweight

jib

cart

The crane's long arm is the **jib.** A cart runs along rails inside it, carrying the cable and hook. **Counterweights** at the other end keep it from toppling over.

The jib is lifted up section by section using a mobile crane (one on a truck).

K1000 tower crane

Maker: Kroll (Denmark)

Total Height: 394 ft (120 m)

Total Weight: Up to 1,102 tons (1,000 t)

Tower Sections: 28 ft by 39 ft (8.5m by 12 m)

Jib Length: Up to 328 ft (100 m)

Load: Up to 110 tons (100 t) standard, 275 tons (250 t) with special equipment

Fixed Counterweight: 110 tons (100 t)

Mobile Counterweights: (2 of 40 t)

Hoist Lift Speed: 164 ft (50 m) per minute for 16.5 tons (15 t)

Glossary

Blade

The long, smooth-edged metal part that cuts or pushes on a bulldozer, leveler, or similar machine.

Boom

The long, moveable, or swinging part of a big machine such as a crane or backhoe.

Cab

The place where a driver or operator sits to control a large vehicle, crane, or similar machine.

Caterpillar track

A long ridged belt in a loop shape that goes around with wheels inside it, used on tanks and big construction vehicles.

Concrete

A mix of cement, sand, small stones, and water, which sets and becomes rock-hard.

Container

Standard-sized steel box with doors at one end, which can be lifted and loaded onto trucks, ships, and railroad cars.

Conveyor belt

A long, endless loop or belt that goes around and carries or conveys items or materials.

Counterweight

A large, heavy block of concrete, metal, or similar material that balances a vehicle's load to keep it from tipping over.

Demolition

Taking apart or knocking down buildings such as houses, factories, and apartment buildings.

Gears

A system of toothed wheels called cogs that come together or mesh in different combinations. They are placed inside a gearbox so a vehicle can go at different speeds for the same engine turning speed.

Hydraulic

Working by the force of a high-pressure liquid, usually water or a special oil.

Jib

The long, arm-like part of a crane or similar machine.

Piston

A solid cylinder or disk that moves under pressure.

Ripper

A claw or claws that dig into the ground and break or rip it apart as they move along, often on the back of a bulldozer.

Tread

The part of a tire that has grooves and bumps that grip the ground.

Web Sites

http://www.pbs.org/wgbh/buildingbig/skyscraper/basics.html

Part of the large Building Big site covering all kinds of huge constructions such as skyscrapers, dams, bridges and tunnels, and the machines that make them.

http://www.buildingconstructionequipment.com/Bulldozer.asp

A big site with details of many construction machines, from cranes to forklifts.

http://science.howstuffworks.com/tower-crane.htm

http://science.howstuffworks.com/

Two of the many construction machines explained by the How Stuff Works people.

http://www.tallestskyscrapers.info/

The world's tallest buildings and how they were made.

Further Reading

Construction Vehicles (How Machines Work) by Terry Jennings, Smart Apple Media, 2009

Forklifts (Machines at Work) by Marv Alinas, Child's World, 2007

Bulldozers (Big Machines) by David and Penny Glover, Smart Apple Media, 2006

Note to Parents and Teachers:

Index